THE OXFORD PIANO METHOD

PIANO TIME CLASS[S]

arranged by

Pauline Hall

CONTENTS

(contd.)

Illustrations by John Taylor

All the pieces in this collection, which have been graded in order of difficulty, are really easy arrangements of the well-known classics. Many of them were originally written for orchestra, opera, or ballet—look out for the original versions on recordings, radio, and TV, and listen to them when you have a chance.

You should always have one or two of these classics up your sleeve as 'party pieces' for you to play to your friends and family—they will thoroughly enjoy listening to the tunes they know and love, and you'll enjoy them too!

P.H.

OXFORD
UNIVERSITY PRESS

Great Clarendon Street, Oxford OX2 6DP, England
198 Madison Avenue, New York, NY10016, USA

Oxford is a registered trademark of Oxford University Press

© Oxford University Press 1994

31st impression

Theme from the 'Pastoral' Symphony

This tune from Beethoven's Sixth Symphony describes a peaceful scene in the countryside.

Ludwig van Beethoven (1770–1827)

Lullaby

Johannes Brahms (1833–97)

Ode to Joy

This tune comes from Beethoven's Choral Symphony, No. 9.

Ludwig van Beethoven (1770–1827)

Theme from the 'Surprise' Symphony

Haydn wrote a great number of symphonies. Many of them have nicknames like 'The Bear' and 'The Hen'. The surprise here is the loud chord in the middle.

Joseph Haydn (1732–1809)

The Blue Danube

This is probably the best-known of the many waltzes that Strauss wrote.

Johann Strauss (1825–99)

Skaters' Waltz

Emil Waldteufel (1837–1915)

'Largo' from the 'New World' Symphony

This beautiful tune is played as a solo by the cor anglais, a member of
the oboe family.

Antonín Dvořák (1841–1904)

Largo

'Spring' from The Four Seasons

Vivaldi lived about the same time as Bach and Handel. His most popular works are four concertos for orchestra, describing the seasons of the year.

Antonio Vivaldi (1678–1741)

'La donna è mobile' from the opera Rigoletto

Giuseppe Verdi (1813–1901)

Dance of the Hours

Amilcare Ponchielli (1834–86)

Radetsky March

Johann Strauss (1804–49)

'Nessun dorma' from the opera Turandot

Just before this aria, the beautiful Princess Turandot has been challenged by Prince Calaf to find out his name by daybreak or she will have to marry him. Here, the Prince is confident that his name will not be discovered, and that Turandot will be his.

Giacomo Puccini (1858–1924)

'William Tell' Overture

William Tell was the last of the thirty six operas that Rossini wrote.

Gioacchino Rossini (1792–1868)

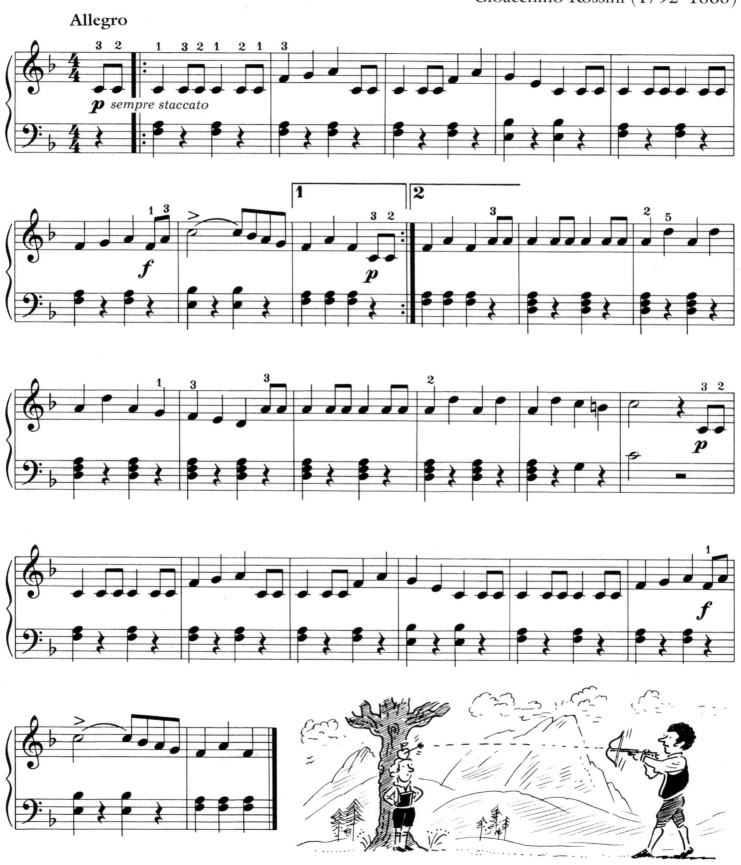

Toreador Song

This is from the opera *Carmen* which is about a beautiful Spanish
gypsy girl and her lover, a popular toreador.

Georges Bizet (1838–75)

See the Conquering Hero Comes

George Frideric Handel (1685–1759)

Für Elise

The title means 'for Elise'. No-one knows who 'Elise' was: however, it could well have been a misreading of Therese (von Brunswick) with whom Beethoven was in love.

Ludwig van Beethoven (1770–1827)

Can-can

This high-spirited can-can must have slow practice if you want to be able to play it up to speed.

Allegro   Jacques Offenbach (1819–80)

17

'March of the Kings' from L'Arlésienne

This is one of the well-known themes from the incidental music written by Bizet for Daudet's play, *L'Arlésienne* ('The Maid of Arles'). Arles is a town in the south of France.

Georges Bizet (1838–75)

'Mazurka' from the ballet Coppélia

A mazurka is a dance from Poland.

Léo Delibes (1836–91)

'Jupiter' from The Planets

Jesu, Joy of Man's Desiring

Bach's chorales (or hymn tunes) were often accompanied by flowing counterpoint. This is played on the organ whilst the choir sings the chorale.

Johann Sebastian Bach (1685–1750)

Waltz from Die Fledermaus

This waltz comes from an operetta (a comic opera) by Strauss.
'Die Fledermaus' means 'The Bat'.

Johann Strauss (1825–99)

Wedding March

Traditionally played as the bride and bridegroom come down the aisle
at the end of the wedding service, this march was originally written for
Shakespeare's *A Midsummer Night's Dream*.

Felix Mendelssohn (1809–47)

The Trout

Schubert wrote a great many songs, and *The Trout* is one of these. He also used the theme from this song in a piano quintet, nicknamed the 'Trout' Quintet.

Franz Schubert (1797–1828)

'Hornpipe' from the Water Music

George Frideric Handel (1685–1759)

Caprice

Paganini was a brilliant violinist. Several composers including Liszt, Brahms, and Rachmaninov 'borrowed' this tune on which to base some of their own compositions.

Niccolò Paganini (1782–1840)

25

'Land of Hope and Glory', Pomp and Circumstance March No. 1

This piece is sung every year at The Last Night of the Proms in The Royal Albert Hall.

Edward Elgar (1857–1934)

Valse des Fleurs

This waltz comes from the music for the ballet *The Nutcracker*.

Pyotr Ilyich Tchaikovsky (1840–93)

Adagio

This famous arrangement, known as Albinoni's Adagio, was in fact
written by the twentieth-century Italian composer Remo Giazotto,
who based the piece on the only remaining fragment— just a few
bars—of Albinoni's original.

Remo Giazotto–Tomaso Albinoni (1671–1750)

Impromptu

Franz Schubert (1797–1828)

Trumpet Tune

Henry Purcell (1659–95)

The trill is played:

Vltava

This piece is describing a river flowing to the sea. It needs careful use
of the sustaining pedal.

Bedřich Smetana (1824–84)

Chanson du Matin

Edward Elgar (1857–1934)

The Arrival of the Queen of Sheba

This exciting, bustling piece was originally written for orchestra.
It needs slow practice to get the fingerwork fast and even.

George Frideric Handel (1685–1759)

Prelude Op. 28, No. 7

This piece is improved if you use the sustaining pedal. Be careful to put the pedal down and lift it up where marked.

Frédéric Chopin (1810–49)

Minuet

This famous minuet comes from a string quartet—Boccherini wrote
over a hundred of these.

Luigi Boccherini (1743–1805)

Theme from the 'Unfinished' Symphony

This symphony is known as the 'Unfinished' because it only has three sections (or movements) instead of the usual four.

Franz Schubert (1797–1828)

'Pizzicato' from the ballet Sylvia

In violin playing, the term 'pizzicato' means that the strings are plucked and not bowed.

Léo Delibes (1836–91)

Nocturne Op. 9, No. 2

A nocturne is a slow piece with a beautiful melody describing the romantic beauty of night. In this piece, the first note in each of the left hand bars is held for the whole bar.

Frédéric Chopin (1810–49)

'The Swan' from Carnival of the Animals

Camille Saint-Saëns (1835–1921)

'Dance of the Sugar Plum Fairy'
from the ballet Nutcracker

Pyotr Ilyich Tchaikovsky (1840–93)

Reproduced and printed by
Halstan & Co. Ltd., Amersham, Bucks., England